AT HOME IN NAZARETH

ON A lovely green hill where the flowers grow, there is a town of white houses. It is called Nazareth. It was the home of the Holy Family, but they had been away for a long time. Now they were coming home again. They walked down the long road and climbed the hill. They went up the street to the house where Mary and Joseph used to live. What do you suppose they found?

ANOTHER family was living in Saint Joseph's house. The Holy Family had to go down the street and look for another house to live in. Was Saint Joseph cross? Certainly not. Jesus and Mary were tired from the long trip. Did they grumble when they had to go and find another house? No! Of course not. God wanted them to live in another house. They wanted to do only what God wanted.

MARY AND JOSEPH made their new home clean and pretty. The Holy Family's little house at Nazareth was a happy home. Nobody was ever grumpy or mad. Nobody was selfish. Everybody helped. They had *such* nice times together.

JESUS always did what Mary and Joseph told Him. He was obedient, because He wanted to please God, His Father. God says to all of us, "Honor your father and your mother." That means obey them and be good to them.

JESUS went to school in Nazareth. There He learned to read and to write. Now remember, Jesus is God's Son. He knows everything, just like God His Father. Why did He go to school and learn with the other children in Nazareth? I think He wanted to show us He was a *real* boy.

THE HOLY Family had plain meals like all their neighbors. They were poor. Why did Jesus want to be poor? He was God's Son, and He could have had the whole world, if He wanted. But Jesus was born in a poor family, to teach us that such things as money, and nice clothes, and houses, and lots of different kinds of food and candy are not one bit important. They cannot make us happy. Jesus wanted to be poor, so that nobody can say He had it easy.

JESUS loved His Mother and Saint Joseph, and He helped at home. He was never lazy. He wanted to show us how to do things the right way. He showed us what right-away obedience is.

JESUS played with other children of Nazareth. They all liked to play with Jesus. They always had fun because Jesus played fair. He waited His turn. What game do you think He is playing here? No matter what Jesus is doing, He is doing it well, so as to please God, His Father in Heaven.

JESUS grew a little taller every day, just like other children, just as you do. Jesus was God's Son; but He ate, and slept, and grew just like you do. He was a real child. He did all the good things that other children did. He often helped His Mother carry water from the well. He ran errands and helped Saint Joseph too.

NOW fold your hands and close your eyes. Think about Jesus. He is listening. Whisper to Him: "Jesus, I love You! Thank You for showing me how to act at home, at play, and at school. Please help me, Jesus, to be like You."

SPINNING-TOP

If you have a very short pencil and an empty spool of thread, you can make yourself a nice spinning-top. Push the pencil through the hole of the spool so that the point sticks out on the other side. Then let it dance by spinning it by the "handle."

You can paint the spool and decorate it with stripes or dots. That will make nice patterns when it moves. If you let it spin on different kinds of paper, or tip it, so that the pencil spins at a slant, your spinning-top will even make different sounds while it whirls around.

CATCH-THE-BALL

To make a Catch-The-Ball, you need a small paper cup, a piece of thin string or ribbon (about seven to eight inches long) and a piece of metal foil. If you don't have metal foil, use one small and one large button instead.

Make a knot in one end of the string and squeeze some metal foil around it, until it dangles like a bead on the end of the string. (Instead of the foil you can use the small button.)

Prick a hole in the bottom of the paper cup. Put the string through, so that the knot is on the inside of the cup, preventing the string from slipping through.

Tie a knot in the other end of the string and shape a little ball around it, with the rest of your metal foil.

The Catch-The-Ball is ready now. You can practice your skill by swinging the ball up into the air, and then trying to catch it in the paper cup.

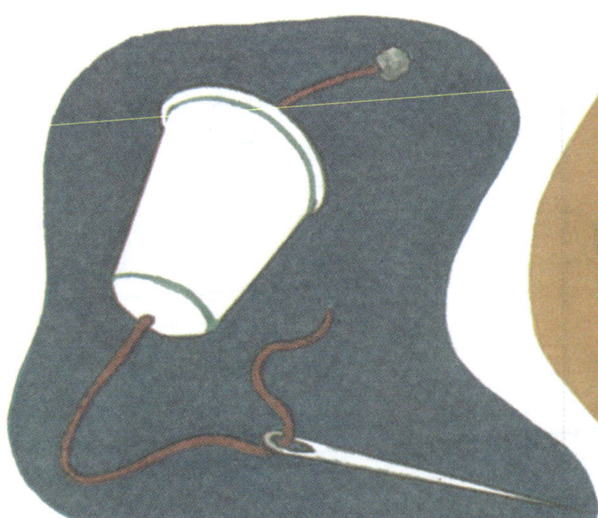

If you do not have a paper cup, you can make one out of any square piece of stiff paper.

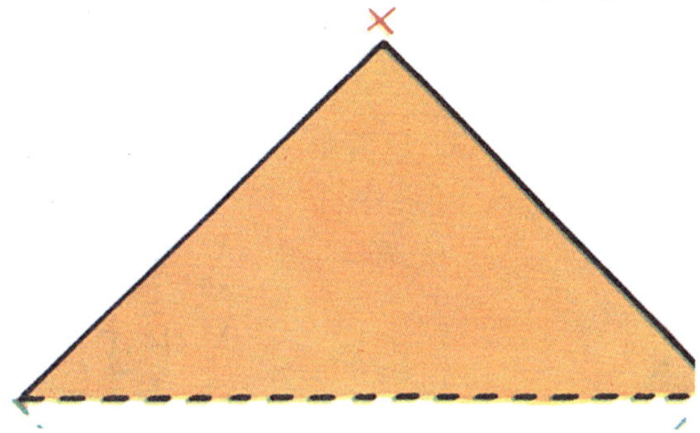

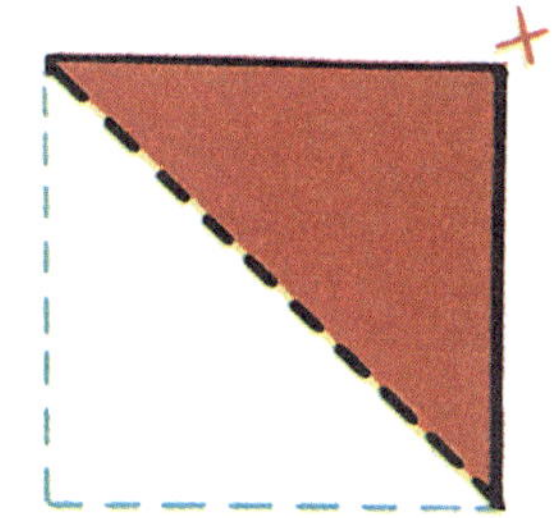

Fold the paper into a triangle.

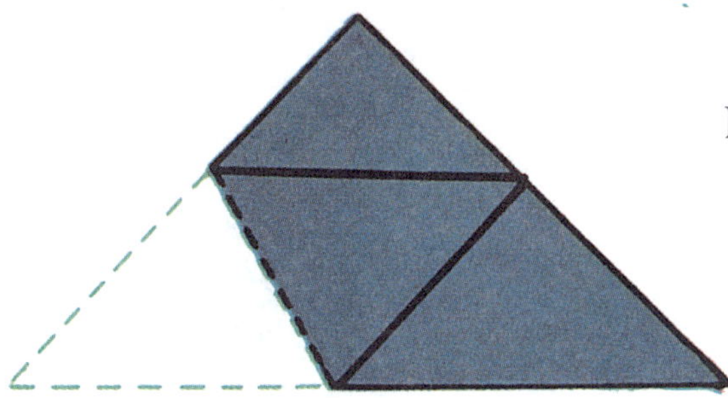

Fold one corner of the long side up, until it touches the edge.

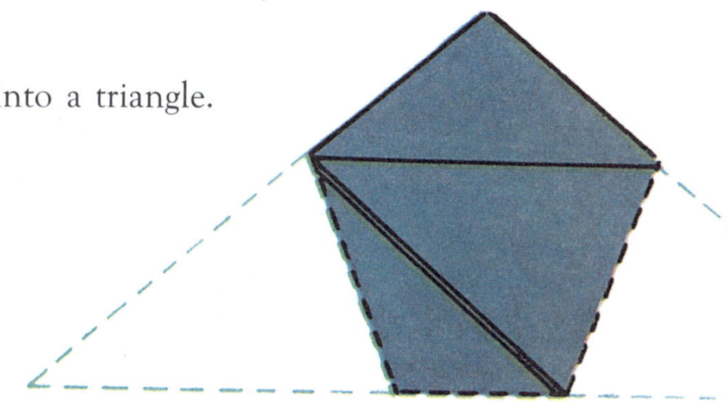

Fold the second corner up the same way.

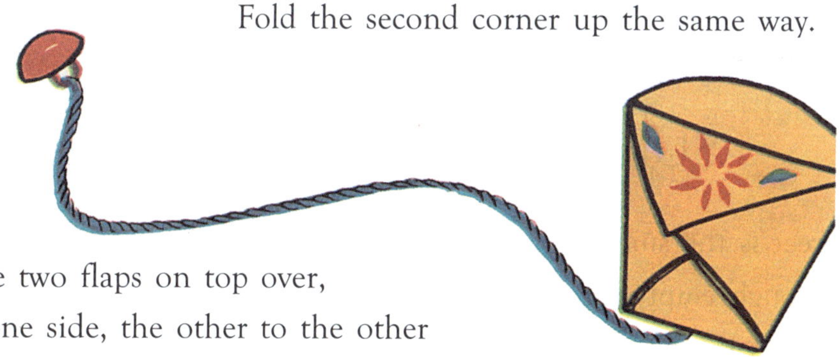

Turn the two flaps on top over, one to one side, the other to the other side. Now open the cup.

SUMMER SUN

Great is the sun and wide he goes
Through empty heaven without repose;
And in the blue and glowing days
More thick than rain he showers his rays.

Though closer still the blinds we pull
To keep the shady parlor cool,
Yet he will find a chink or two
To slip his golden fingers through.

The dusty attic spider clad
He, through the keyhole maketh glad;
And through the broken edge of tiles,
Into the laddered hay-loft smiles.

Meantime his golden face around
He bares to all the garden ground,
And sheds a warm and glittering look
Among the ivy's inmost nook.

Above the hills, along the blue,
Round the bright air with footing true,
To please the child, to paint the rose,
The gardener of the world, he goes.

Robert Louis Stevenson

THE GIANT

There once lived a  with an enormous appetite. For breakfast he drank a tankful of 

and ate a ful of 

and a hundred , boiled in a  as big as a . He also ate two slices of  the size of a 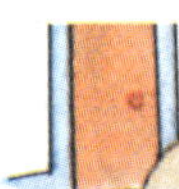, with a carload of 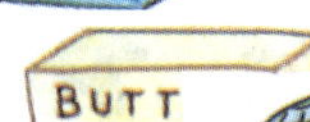

and 

spread between. After breakfast the 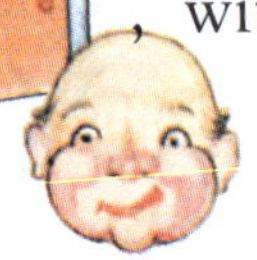 walked around the  to work up an appetite for lunch. When he came back his appetite was enormous. He ate a  as long as a  and a  of salad made with enough  to feed a million . He finished up with an  that stood taller than a . After that he went shopping for dinner. Can you imagine what he ate for dinner? It was so much that even a schoolteacher would not be able to remember it all!

WUPSY AND THE STORM DEVIL

There were often big storms at Matongu which filled the rivers and streams with water and made the banana trees grow up almost while you watched.

But once there was a Great Storm which the people of Matongu still speak of in hushed voices. Some whisper because they are afraid the storm spirits will hear and be angry and come again. But the Christians say a prayer from the Litanies: "From all tempests and wars, deliver us, O Lord."

It was just before the rainy season. For three months the sun had been shining all day long. The fields were dry and parched, the grass on the roofs of the huts snapped if you touched it and wooden beams cracked wide open!

The new church stood proudly on top of the hill, its doors wide open to all the people of Matongu and the other villages of the forest. Father George and Father Christopher and Brother Bill were all proud of their work. Perhaps, as Father Christopher said afterwards, they were *too* proud of it. The devils often come along when we are most proud of our work and pleased with ourselves.

Anyway, it certainly was the Storm Devil who came that day. During the morning the air seemed as still and as hot as the air in an oven. The birds of the forest stopped singing and went to hide in their nests or in the corners of the thick branches. All the animals, big and little, lay down in their lairs, fearful of what might come. The people of Matongu looked up at the sky and shook their heads anxiously. The Guardian Angels consulted

together. Then suddenly, without a sound or breath of wind, the topmost branches of the tallest trees began to wave to and fro.

Father George, looking from his window on the hill, saw dense black clouds coming over the distant mountains. Then he saw long jagged streaks of lightning and heard the distant rumble of thunder.

Ntaka-Ntaka called Sunny into the hut.

The branches of the trees waved, and a breath of chill wind could be felt down below. The breath grew to a breeze, and the breeze to a great wind which came rushing on Matongu. The wind seemed to blow from all sides at once. It roared in and out of the huts, tearing at the grass roofs and pulling at the wooden poles. It rushed in and out of the banana plantations, until first one tree and then another was almost stripped of its leaves, then uprooted and thrown on the ground. The mighty giant trees of the forest that would not bend before it were flung down with a great crash.

The people crouching in their huts heard them fall one by one. Up on the hill the church stood sturdy and proud, but suddenly a fierce gust of wind blew round the roof, lifted it right off, and it crashed down upon the huts of the village. And all the time the rain poured down in great heavy sheets, soaking into the parched ground, then making little lakes all over the place, while overhead the thunder crashed and rolled.

What were the Angels doing all this time? They were busy making sure the storm devil did not do any more harm than he was allowed to. They were busy keeping the people of Matongu safe, making sure that the house of the missioners did not fall down too, and lots of other things.

Wupsy spent this time looking after Sunny, for his hut was one of those on which the roof of the church fell. The pole in the middle of the hut broke right in two, and down came the roof with a terrible crash. If Wupsy had not been watching, the pole might have fallen right on Sunny. But Wupsy spread his wings over Sunny so that the bits of falling roof did not hurt him at all.

It was indeed a terrible storm, but it was over in less than a quarter of an hour. Soon the sun was shining again, the birds were singing in the trees and the people of Matongu began to peek out from their torn and ragged huts.

Up on the hill, Father George and Brother Bill came out to look at the church. They both looked at it for a moment without saying anything, then Father George said: "Brother Bill, I think you will have to put a new roof on our church."

Brother Bill simply grunted, which might have meant anything. Then they both ran down into the village to help the people in the ruined huts.

The Angels had been busy, and to prove it, the people of Matongu crawled out from their huts with hardly a scratch on them. A few drops of iodine from Father George's medicine box was all that anyone needed.

That evening the missioners talked it over together.

"Well," said Father Christopher, "that was a storm! There has been a lot of damage, but fortunately nobody has been hurt."

"No," said Father George, "and it will take them only a few days to build their huts again. What about the church, Brother?"

"I've been all over it very carefully," replied Brother Bill. "The walls are still solid, and it will be easy to put a new roof on. What's more, the other day I came across some clay that will make splendid tiles, so we can have a real tile roof now. It would have taken a long time to get that straw roof off, so the storm has really been a help."

Down in the village, some of the people were talking: "Ah! Was that a storm! When we tell our grandchildren about this they won't believe it." "They would not believe anyone could live through such a storm!" "Did you know that a new spring has come up among the rocks down on the banana plantation?" "A lot of good came from that storm!"

The storm devil was rather upset when he found that little damage had been done, and that the people were pleased and happier than before! He sat under a tree and gnawed at his tail in spite, till he saw, high in the treetops, a Guardian Angel praising God.

Then he bit a piece right out of his tail and fled far away over the mountains.

Wupsy will be back again in Issue 20. Watch for him.